Marie Cahill

JG PRESS

Published in the USA 1994 by JG Press
Distributed by World Publications, Inc.

The JG Press imprint is a trademark of
JG Press, Inc.
455 Somerset Avenue
North Dighton, MA 02764

Produced by
Brompton Books Corporation
15 Sherwood Place
Greenwich, Connecticut 06830

ISBN 1-57215-032-7

Printed in Slovenia

CONTENTS

Photo Credits

All photos courtesy of American Graphic Sys-
tems Archives except those listed below:
© RE DeJauregui 63 (bottom)
Las Vegas News Bureau 42 (bottom), 49
   (bottom)
Mississippi Department of Economic Devel-
   opment 11 (bottom)
Tennessee Tourist Development 60 (all), 61
   (all), 62
© Bill Yenne 63 (top)

Page 1: Elvis stares sincerely to cam-
era left, on the set of one of his many
Metro-Goldwyn-Mayer motion
pictures.
Page 2: Elvis thrills his fans during
the famous 'comeback special' of
1968.
These pages, left—In an all-out dance
number from the movie *Jailhouse
Rock*, Elvis cut a flamboyant figure—
and *right*—with a coterie of fans, circa
1956.

Designed by Ruth DeJauregui

INTRODUCTION

Born on 8 January 1935, in Tupelo, Mississippi, Elvis was one of a set of twins born to Vernon Elvis Presley and Gladys Love Presley. From the very beginning, Elvis Aron Presley was a survivor: his brother, Jesse Garon Presley, died six hours after birth. As a boy, Elvis enjoyed singing in the East Heights Assembly of God Church. He first performed publicly while in fifth grade, singing 'Old Shep' on WELO radio, as a reward for taking second place in a talent contest.

The family moved to Memphis, Tennessee, where Elvis attended OC Hume High School. While driving a truck for the Crown Electric Company, Elvis stopped by Sun Records' Memphis Recording Services, where he paid four dollars to record two songs—'My Happiness' and 'That's When Your Heartache Begins.' He returned there in January 1954 to record 'Casual Love Affair' and I'll Never Stand in Your Way.' This time, Sam Phillips, the head of Sun Records, liked what he heard, and a legendary singing career began.

His recordings mounted up, and he became a regional phenomenon, then a national and an international phenomenon. After television appearances on the Dorsey brothers' *Stage Show* and the *Milton Berle Show*, Elvis signed a contract with Hal Wallis of Paramount Pictures to star in three motion pictures. Elvis was to make further television appearances on the Steve Allen, Jackie Gleason and Ed Sullivan variety shows.

Among his early hit songs were 'Mystery Train' (1954) and 'That's All Right, Mama' (1954) (both with Sun Records); 'I Got a Woman,' 'Money, Honey,' 'Heartbreak Hotel,' 'Lawdy Miss Clawdy,' 'Shake, Rattle and Roll,' 'Tutti Frutti' and 'Blue Suede Shoes' (all January of 1956, with RCA Records); 'Jailhouse Rock,' 'All Shook Up,' 'Let Me Be Your Teddy Bear' and 'Too Much' (all 1957, with RCA); plus RCA renditions of 'All Shook Up' and 'It's Now or Never.'

In fact, Elvis recorded three dozen tracks in late 1956, many of which were released during his two-year tour of duty with the US Army at the end of the decade. These included 'Love Me Tender,' 'Don't Be Cruel,' 'Ready Teddy,' 'Rip It Up,' 'Long Tall Sally' and his greatest hit *ever*: 'You Ain't Nothin' But a Hound Dog.'

His acting future lay in motion pictures, however, and since Paramount had no immediate project for

Elvis, Hal Wallis arranged a deal with the Twentieth Century-Fox studios, and thereafter handled many of Elvis' 'movie deals.'

Elvis' first film for Fox was to be *Love Me Tender*, co-starring Richard Egan and Deborah Paget. Released on 16 November 1956, it was a smash hit. Through the years, he would star in 30 motion pictures, among which were *Loving You* (Paramount, 1957); *Jailhouse Rock* (Metro-Goldwyn-Mayer, 1957); *King Creole* (Paramount, 1958); *GI Blues* (Paramount, 1960); *Flaming Star* (Twentieth Century-Fox, 1960); *Wild in the Country* (Twentieth Century-Fox, 1961); *Blue Hawaii* (Paramount, 1961); *Follow That Dream* (United Artists, 1962); *Kid Galahad* (United Artists, 1962); *Girls! Girls! Girls!* (Paramount, 1962); *It Happened at the World's Fair* (Metro-Goldwyn-Mayer, 1962); *Fun in Acapulco* (Hal Wallis Productions, 1962); *Kissin' Cousins* (Metro-Goldwyn-Mayer, 1964); *Viva Las Vegas* (Metro-Goldwyn-Mayer, 1964); *Paradise, Hawaiian Style* (Paramount, 1966); *Spinout* (Metro-Goldwyn-Mayer, 1966); *Easy Come, Easy Go* (Paramount, 1967); *Double Trouble* (Metro-Goldwyn-Mayer, 1967); *Clambake* (United Artists, 1967); *Stay Away, Joe* (Metro-Goldwyn-Mayer, 1968); *Speedway* (Metro-Goldwyn-Mayer, 1968); *Live a Little, Love a Little* (Metro-Goldwyn-Mayer, 1968); *Charro!* (National General Productions, Inc, 1969); and *The Trouble With Girls* (Metro-Goldwyn-Mayer, December 1969); *Change of Habit* (NBC-Universal, January 1970).

There were also documentaries such as *Elvis: That's the Way It Is* (Metro-Goldwyn-Mayer, 1970) and *Elvis on Tour* (Metro-Goldwyn-Mayer, 1972), plus a number of television specials, including *Aloha From Hawaii* (1973).

With the revival of his live performance career in 1968, Elvis again began turning out the hit records, as is discussed later in this book. When he died in 1977, Elvis Presley was 42, and yet had lived a life that would require most men several full lifetimes to live. In his worldwide community of fans, he lives on.

Facing page: Elvis Aron Presley had an impoverished childhood that was rich in his parents' love. When he died a wealthy man on 16 August 1977, the world lost one of its greatest entertainers.

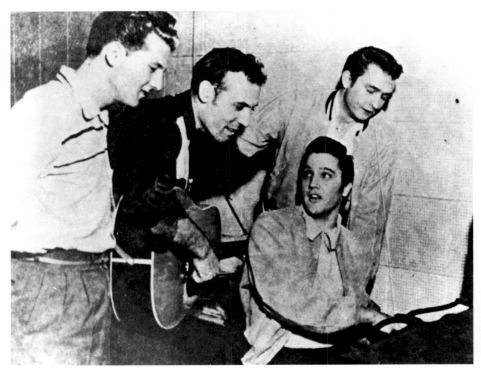

Elvis on the Rise

After signing a three-year contract with Sun Records on 19 July 1954, Elvis began his climb. *Above left:* Elvis with his beloved mother, Gladys Love Presley. *At far left:* In full swing as the 'Hillbilly Cat' on the local variety show, *Louisiana Hay Ride*, in 1955.

Elvis' peers were also legendary. *At left:* In the Sun studios—(left to right) Jerry Lee Lewis, Carl Perkins, Elvis, and Johnny Cash. *Above:* The rising star maintains his image. *At right:* The clothes were a part of it all—not to mention blue suede shoes.

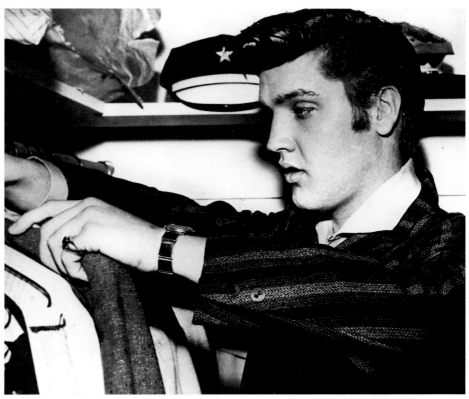

The Soft Light of Home

Elvis' face was tailor-made for soft-lit promotional photos: he seemed so at home in them. *At left:* Elvis lambent, with guitar.

As a performer, he was brilliant in any light *(above)*, but in his heart remained one true home *(at right)*, the little house his father built in Tupelo, Mississippi.

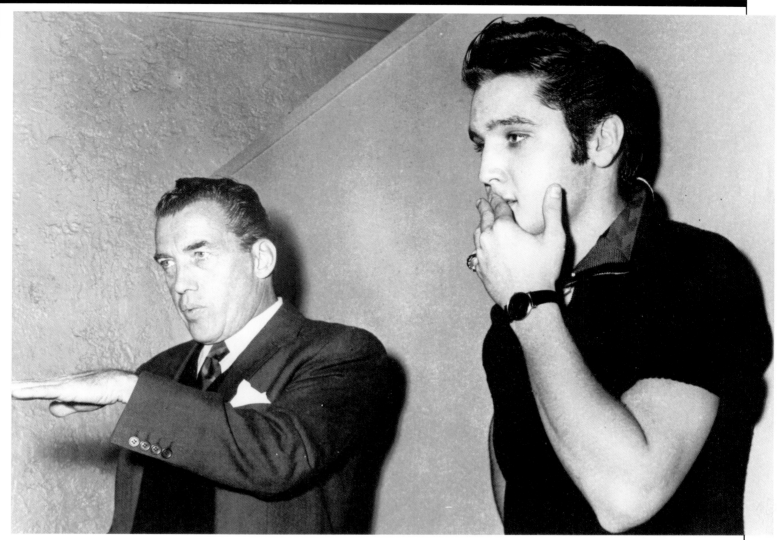

Elvis Meets Television

Elvis was a sensation during a western skit on the *Steve Allen Show* in 1956—*at right*, left to right: Andy Griffith, Imogene Coca, Elvis and Steve Allen. He was downright controversial in his appearances on Ed Sullivan's *Toast of the Town (above)*; but seemed to swing with those 'Kings of Swing,' Tommy and Jimmy Dorsey *(above left)* on their *Stage Show* in 1956.

He went from riveting to wild in his live performances *(at left, both)*.

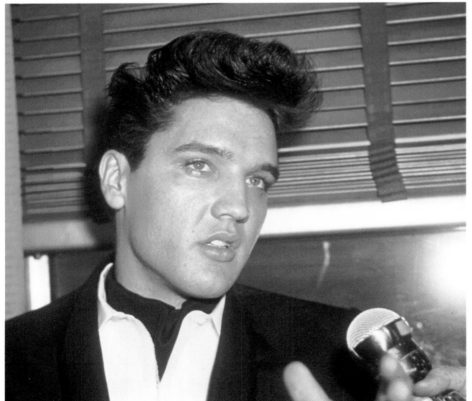

The Hillbilly Sophisticate

By 1957, Elvis Presley was internationally acclaimed, yet the publicity was both a source of pride and meditative wonderment for him. *At left and above:* Elvis at the microphone, and in a thoughtful mood.

His wealth was such that in March, 1957, he gave his mother a $100,000 mansion where the Presley family could live together. This mansion was to be called Graceland. *At right:* Elvis at Graceland.

On the Silver Screen

Elvis starred in 30 motion pictures. *At left:* Elvis and Deborah Paget in *Love Me Tender* (1956). *At right:* Elvis solo, and with Lizabeth Scott *(above)* and Dolores Hart *(above right)* in *Loving You* (1957).

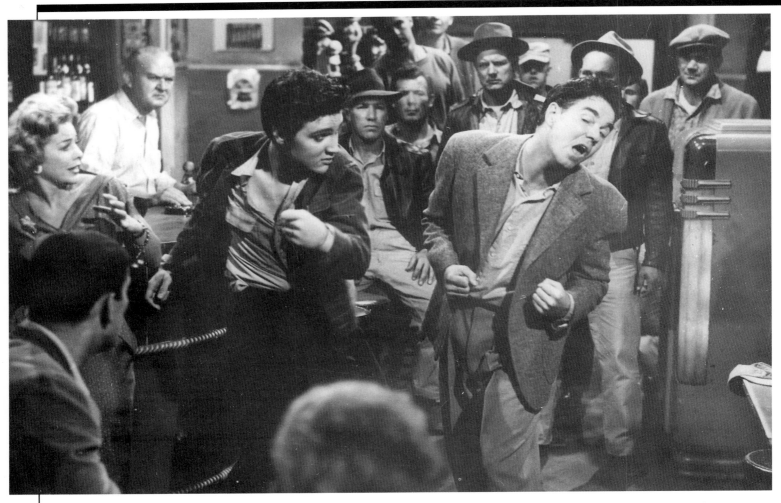

Jailhouse Rock

Elvis, as Vince Everett, slays a bully *(above left)*, and is arrested *(at left)*. *Above and top right:* 'Everybody in the whole cellblock/ was dancin' to the jailhouse rock....' Elvis/Vince was convincingly surrounded by adoring fans *(above right)*, and found true love with co-star Judy Tyler, as Peggy Van Alden *(at right)*.

King Creole

At left: Elvis as Danny Fisher and Carolyn Jones as 'Ronnie' in *King Creole* (1958). *Above:* Elvis/Danny in a fighting pose.

Above right: He wears an 'eat your heart out' look as he is kissed by co-stars Dolores Hart and Ms Jones.

At right: Elvis/Danny confronts Walter Matthau, as the notorious Maxie Fields, in an electrifying scene.

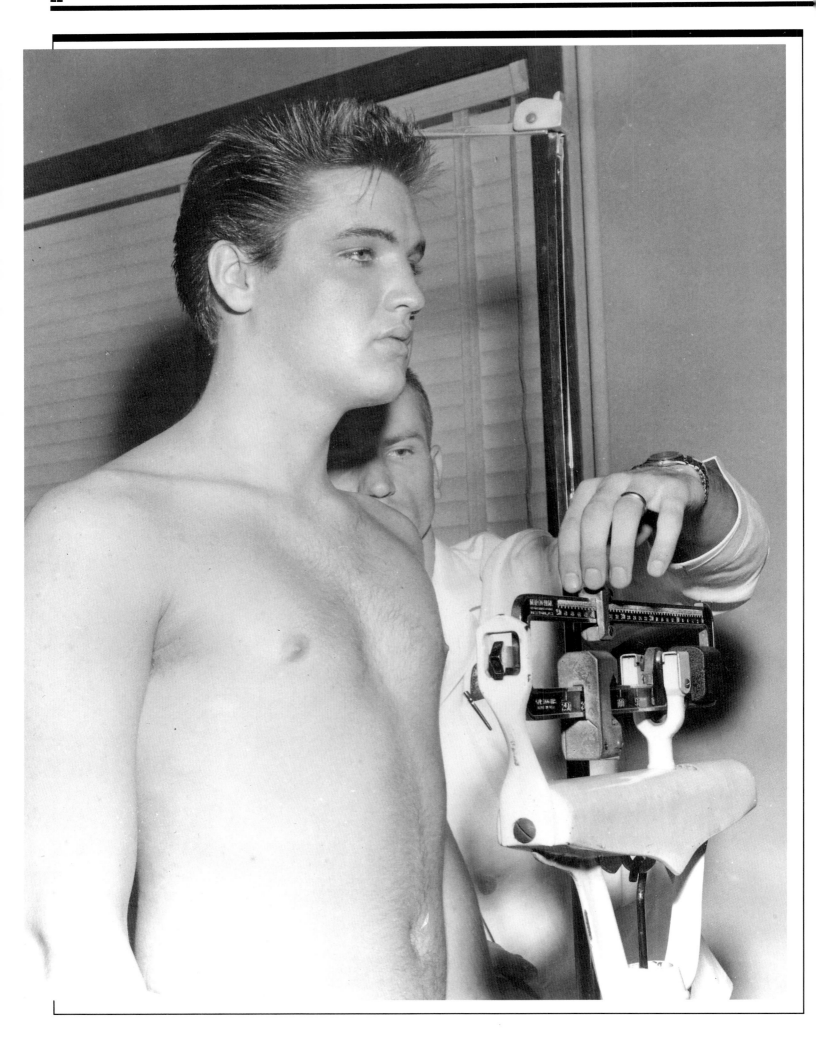

In the Army Now

On 24 March 1958, Elvis was accompanied to the Memphis Armed Forces Induction Center to begin serving a draft-mandated term in the US Army.

He volunteered for regular duty, as opposed to a special entertainment unit, and spent a two-year stint at a military installation in West Germany, attaining the rank of Sergeant.

On these pages are views of Elvis' Army experience.

World's Most Famous GI

Above: Sergeant Elvis Presley very happily fields 'media flak' upon his discharge in March 1960.

Colonel Parker was close at hand upon Elvis' discharge, as is evidenced by the photo *at left*.

At right: Elvis waves 'goodbye to all that,' and hello to resuming his career. His stay in West Germany had one lasting effect on his life—he had Priscilla Beaulieu there.

Flaming Blues

This page: Elvis, reprising his military experience, as Tulsa MacLean in *GI Blues* (1960). *At right:* He evinced a much different persona as Pacer Burton in *Flaming Star* (1960).

Wild in Hawaii

This page: Elvis Presley, as Glenn Tyler, and Tuesday Weld, as 'Noreen,' in scenes from *Wild in the Country* (1961).

At right: Elvis and a bevy of female extras in a promotion still for *Blue Hawaii* (1961), which gave him a limited chance to don his old Army uniform *(above far right)*.

Elvis portrayed Chad Gates, who is seen *at above right* with one of his paramours in the film.

Many Elvises

Facing page: Elvis, co-stars and a special-effects double in *Kissin' Cousins* (1964). *Above, both:* Elvis and a young co-star in *It Happened at the World's Fair* (1962). *At left:* Elvis as Walter Gulick in *Kid Galahad* (1962).

Viva Las Vegas

These pages: Elvis and co-star Ann-Margret in their roles as 'Lucky' and 'Rusty,' respectively, in the April 1964 release of *Viva Las Vegas* (1964).

Elvis, as 'Lucky,' was an aspiring race car driver, and Ann-Margret's 'Rusty' was a swimming instructor. Songs include a duet, 'The Lady Loves Me,' featuring the two stars.

Three Light Films

Facing page: Elvis as Johnny Tyronne in *Harum Scarum* (1965).

Above: Elvis and supporting cast in *Paradise, Hawaiian Style* (1966).

At right: A publicity still for *Roustabout* (1964), in which Elvis played a carnival jack-of-all-trades named Charlie Rogers.

Double Trouble

Above and at left: Scenes from *Double Trouble* (1967), in which Elvis portrayed disco singer Guy Lambert, an otherwise happy-go-lucky fellow who is pursued through Belgium by a literal mob of people—some of whom love him and some of whom want to kill him. Also shown here is co-star Annette Day, as Jill Conway.

At right: In *Clambake* (1967), Elvis played Scott Heyward, a millionaire.

Charro!

These pages: Elvis in costume as reformed outlaw Jess Wade in *Charro!* (1969), with supporting cast and love interest, 'Tracie,' who was portrayed by Ina Balin.

This film is the only motion picture in which Elvis sported a beard. The fighting pose fits one of Elvis' personal interests—he had been a fan of martial arts since his days in the US Army, when he took his first lessons with an instructor in West Germany.

Sweet Memories

While motion pictures took up most of his time in the 1960s, Elvis longed to return to live performance in front of screaming, enthusiastic, fans.

Even as he worked on such films as *Clambake*, *Double Trouble* and *Charro!*, scenes of his earlier career—and the closeness to his adoring fans that he then enjoyed—washed through his mind.

These pages: A younger Elvis with his fans.

Three of Them

Elvis Presley had courted Priscilla Beaulieu since August 1959. They were married at 9:41 am on 1 May 1967 in Las Vegas. *Above right:* Elvis and Priscilla, just after exchanging marital vows. *At left:* The newlyweds prepare to cut their cake at the reception. *Above:* The rice rains down on Mr and Mrs Elvis Presley.

On 1 February 1968, Priscilla gave birth to Lisa Marie Presley at Memphis' Baptist Memorial Hospital. *At right:* Lisa Marie and her mom and dad emerge from the hospital.

The Good Old Days

In the late-1960s, Elvis' fans prepared for the return of an Elvis they hadn't seen since the 1950s—a performer who shook the world with his dramatic pop renditions.

Above: Elvis at the microphone in the Sun Records studios, in one of his earliest recording sessions, circa 1954. His first hit was 'That's All Right, Mama.'

At left: Taking a breather during a session. *Facing page:* Charisma to burn, and a much-imitated pose.

Elvis Comes Back

His millions of fans also wanted to see Elvis live—and singing. He made his comeback on the concert stage via television.

The show was taped between 27 and 29 June 1968, and was aired on 3 December of that same year. It was a smash hit, and was proof of Elvis' blossoming forth as a musician once again. *These pages:* scenes from his comeback special.

The special featured the brand-new million seller 'If I Can Dream,' and a plethora of such Elvis classics as 'Heartbreak Hotel,' 'Don't Be Cruel,' 'Jailhouse Rock' and 'Are You Lonesome Tonight?'

On Stage Again

At left: A fan photo from his come-back special. *Above right:* Yet another flamboyant outfit.

He wanted to tour. Colonel Parker set up a contract with Las Vegas' International Hotel for 56 shows in 28 days in July 1969. Opening night was his first strictly live performance in nine years, featuring 'All Shook Up,' 'Blue Suede Shoes,' 'Tiger Man,' 'In the Ghetto' and other songs that were a cross-section of his musical career.

It was a triumph. *At right:* A marquee from one of Elvis' many subsequent Las Vegas stints.

Celebrity

Above: Elvis during a break from one of his late-1960s movies. *At far right:* Elvis in his car, surrounded by his fans, circa 1957.

He was a fan of policemen and criminology. On 21 December 1970, he scribbled a request to be made a federal narcotics officer, handed it to a White House security guard, and was immediately admitted to see US President Richard Nixon — who granted his request *(at right)*.

At left: Emblems of a lifetime of achievement, at Graceland. *Above right:* Elvis and Vernon, his dad.

The Way It Was

Facing page: Elvis, on tour, as represented in *Elvis: That's the Way It Is* (1970), one of two documentaries.

During its filming, Elvis recorded four songs: 'Snowbird,' 'Whole Lotta Shakin' Goin' On,' 'Rags to Riches' and 'Where Did They Go, Lord?'

His concert song selection eventually included 'Proud Mary,' 'Polk Salad Annie,''Bridge Over Troubled Water,' 'Let Me Be There' and the 'American Trilogy' medley of 'Dixie,' 'The Battle Hymn of the Republic' and 'All My Trials.'

This page: Two scenes from *Elvis on Tour*, the second of the 'on tour' documentaries, which won the Golden Globe Award for Best Documentary of 1972.

Aloha

Above and at left: Elvis in performance. In the 1970s, his live concerts were all sold out, and his television specials reached vast audiences. For instance, his *Aloha From Hawaii* show of 14 January 1973 was simulcast from Honolulu to 40 countries worldwide, with an estimated 500 million viewers.

With hits like 'Big Boss Man' and 'Burnin' Love,' Elvis' sound filled the airwaves again. Even so, it was painful for him at times. He and Priscilla—his true love and the mother of their only child—divorced on 9 October 1973. *Facing page:* On location for *Aloha From Hawaii.*

How Great Is Great

These pages: Elvis at work, with a fan and taking a break. Rock stars universally acknowledge his influence: 'Without Elvis,' said Buddy Holly, 'none of us could have made it.' 'That Elvis, man....wrote the book,' says Bruce Springsteen.

Elvis won the first of his four Grammy Awards in 1967 for the gospel album *How Great Thou Art*, which went on to win an unusual *second* Grammy in 1974. Another gospel album, *He Touched Me*, won him another Grammy in 1972.

Elvis also won The Bing Crosby Award of 1971—a special Grammy 'for creative contributions of outstanding artistic or scientific significance.'

Memphis Press-Scimitar

U.S. WEATHER FORECAST: A 60 per cent chance of rain with high in the upper 80s.   Low tonight low 70s. High Thursday mid 80s.

85TH YEAR   MEMPHIS, TENN, WEDNESDAY, AUGUST 17, 1977   TELEPHONES

SPECIAL EDITION

Memphis Leads the World in Mourning the Monarch of Rock 'n Roll

A Lonely Life Ends on Elvis Presley Boulevard

A Tribute to Elvis

The unexpected death of rock 'n roll star Elvis Presley Aug. 16, 1977, was news of international impact. Almost every news agency in the world reported the tragedy under a Memphis dateline.

The public interest required that many members of The Press-Scimitar staff have a hand in compiling and presenting the story. Every conceivable angle was covered in a period of five publication days. Requests for copies of The Press-Scimitar containing coverage of the singer's death poured in from all over the world in great numbers. It was impossible to meet the demand.

Therefore, as a public service to its readers, The Press-Scimitar has reprinted in this special tribute edition all Elvis Presley stories and pictures published in the five-day period. With as few changes as possible, all stories and pictures that we published in the regular editions of The Press-Scimitar are reprinted herein. This edition plus a similar edition of The Commercial Appeal are offered to readers for 50 cents.

ELVIS PRESLEY: THE BEAT WENT ON — AND ON, AND ON

Mourners In Waiting For Last Homecoming Of Revered Singer

Tribute Begins to Flow Freely For Pioneer of Rock 'n Roll
(Aug. 17, 1977)

Death Sets Off Run at Record Stores
(Aug. 17, 1977)

Elvis Presley records were fast selling, selling today off the shelves of record stores across the nation.

Hank Caldwell, manager of the Record Theatre in Buffalo, N.Y., which only used as the "World's Largest Record Store," described the demand for Elvis records as "incredible."

"People are asking for the complete catalogs on him. Our stock has taken up hard to us at all entertainment. The phone has been ringing off the hook with people asking if we have his records. We normally carry a complete stock only because he was the kind of entertainer who will always be sold."

Presley's single records and albums, which sold by the millions and made him a superstar many times over, were perhaps made more popular — because of his death. Many became valuable — because of his death Tuesday.

A UPI survey of records stores throughout the country revealed a rush on existing stocks. Stores scrambled to place orders with distributors for fresh albums, tapes and singles.

Dan Robinson of the Record Bar in Greenville, S.C., said his supply of Elvis records and tapes was sold out in 10 minutes today.

They bought everything we had. We had 15 players, 11 eight-tracks, 26 singles. Pickwick (a distributor) in Atlanta told us they could not fill our order because they were committed to filling more orders than they had stock.

At Peaches, a large record store in Fort Lauderdale, Fla., night manager Susan Vos testified sold they sold $500 worth of Presley albums within hours after the news of his death.

Carter Pays Tribute to Elvis
(Aug. 18, 1977)

WASHINGTON (UPI) — President Carter said today Elvis Presley "permanently changed the face of American popular culture" and became a worldwide symbol of his country's "vitality, rebelliousness and good humor."

The President in a statement issued by the White House on Presley's death, said the popular singer was "unique" and is "irreplaceable."

"Elvis Presley's death deprives our country of a part of itself," Carter said.

OVERCOME BY GRIEF FROM SEEING ELVIS
An unidentified woman receives assistance after she viewed body of singer.

He Gave It All

Elvis did extended stints in Las Vegas, his concert 'home,' and became somewhat of a fixture there, while also maintaining a grueling 'road' schedule—between 17 March 1975 and 1 January 1976, for instance, he toured 74 cities.

It all came to an end with his death on 16 August 1977—an event that filled front pages locally (*facing page*) and around the world. *Above and at right, both:* Visions of the Elvis that fans knew and loved.

Graceland

Located near US Highway 51 on the south side of Memphis, Graceland and its extensive grounds are a landmark for Elvis fans the world over. With a wealth of memorabilia from the great moments of an unforgettable life, Graceland has become a monument to Elvis Presley. *These pages:* Views of Graceland.

ELVIS ARON PRESLEY

Elvis Presley was born in Tupelo, Mississippi on January 8, 1935, the son of Vernon and Gladys Presley. He moved to Memphis in 1948. Soon after signing a contract with Sun Records in 1954 he achieved tremendous popularity. His musical and acting career in records, movies, television, and concerts made him one of the most successful and outstanding entertainers in the world. He died on August 16, 1977 and is buried here at his Memphis home, Graceland.

In Memoriam

Facing page: Elvis' grave at Graceland, a site that is visited by thousands yearly—note that the spelling of his middle name here is actually a *misspelling*, for public relations purposes.

At right: Elvis' star shines bright on Hollywood Boulevard, in company with those of other great entertainers. He was *and is* so special to his fans that many refuse to believe that he is 'gone' in any literal sense of the word.

Above: A young fan poses by a plaque that only hints at the true story of Elvis Presley.

INDEX